Searchlight
BOOKS™

Fear Fest

Frightful Ghost Ships

James Roland

Lerner Publications • Minneapolis

Lerner Publications Company
A division of Lerner Publishing Group, Inc.
241 First Avenue North
Minneapolis, MN 55401 USA

For reading levels and more information, look up this title
at www.lernerbooks.com.

Library of Congress Cataloging-in-Publication Data

Library of Congress Cataloging-in-Publication Data

Names: Roland, James, author.
Title: Frightful ghost ships / James Roland.
Description: Minneapolis : Lerner Publications, 2017. | Series: Searchlight Books™ —
    Fear fest | Includes bibliographical references and index.
Identifiers: LCCN 2016050432 (print) | LCCN 2017006206 (ebook) |
    ISBN 9781512434026 (lb : alk. paper) | ISBN 9781512456059 (pb : alk. paper) |
    ISBN 9781512450767 (eb pdf)
Subjects: LCSH: Ghosts—Juvenile literature. | Shipwrecks—Miscellanea—Juvenile
    literature.
Classification: LCC BF1486 .R65 2017 (print) | LCC BF1486 (ebook) |
    DDC 133.1/22—dc23

LC record available at https://lccn.loc.gov/2016050432

Manufactured in the United States of America
1-42038-23908-1/31/2017

Contents

Chapter 1
MYSTERIOUS MARINERS ... page 4

Chapter 2
NO LONGER SHIPWRECKED ... page 11

Chapter 3
FLAMING SHIPS ... page 18

Chapter 4
GHOST SHIPS ON SCHEDULE ... page 24

Believe It or Not! • 29
Glossary • 30
Learn More about Ghost Ships • 31
Index • 32

MYSTERIOUS MARINERS

Sailors have steered ships through winding rivers and across stormy seas for hundreds of years. For almost as long, there have been stories of ghost ships that appear suddenly and then vanish without a trace. Although many people have tried to explain what has happened to these ghostly ships, nobody can truly say what they are or where they come from.

Old legends tell of well-known ghost ships. Can you name a famous ghost ship?

A Popular Tale

Perhaps the world's most famous ghost ship is the *Flying Dutchman*. For hundreds of years, sailors have reported seeing the *Flying Dutchman*'s strange glowing light and even a crew of skeletons piloting the ship. The tale has become so popular that the *Flying Dutchman* has been featured in many books, movies, and television shows.

The movie *Pirates of the Caribbean: Dead Man's Chest* features the legend of the *Flying Dutchman*.

Some people say the captain of the *Flying Dutchman* is being punished forever for his pride.

The *Flying Dutchman* set sail in the mid-seventeenth century, but the ship never reached its destination. No one knows exactly what happened, but it is thought that one night there was a big storm. The captain kept going through the bad weather until the whole crew died.

People believe that the captain of the ship is forced to sail the seas forever. They say that he tries to lure other ships into rocks and bring bad luck to other sailors.

Since that storm, the crews of countless ships and witnesses on land have said they spotted the *Flying Dutchman*. Sometimes these sightings have been deadly.

In 1881, sailors aboard the HMS *Bacchante* are said to have seen the *Flying Dutchman*. The first crew member to notice the ghostly ship fell to his death seven hours later. This tale and many others like it have led some sailors to believe that seeing the *Flying Dutchman* means bad luck is coming.

The HMS *Bacchante* was a British navy ship.

Fact or Fiction?

Some people say that drowned sailors end up in a place called Davy Jones's locker—but was Davy Jones a real person?

Maybe he was, and maybe he wasn't!

Some historians think the name Davy Jones is based on Saint David, the patron saint of Wales. Welsh sailors would have spoken of the saint when they were trying to make it through dangerous conditions at sea. Or the name could have come from a pirate who forced his captives to walk the plank. His victims would end up dead at the bottom of the sea.

No matter where the name comes from, Davy Jones's locker is definitely not a place you would want to see for yourself.

Over the years, many sailors have perished at sea.

Party aboard a Ghost Ship

A much different type of ghost ship is said to sail around the southern part of South America. The people of Chiloé Island tell the story of *el Caleuche*, a ship that seems to have a party in full swing on its main deck! Witnesses have said that they can hear music and laughter as the ghost ship *el Caleuche* sails around the island.

El Caleuche is thought to be able to travel underwater.

Do you believe that sisters Chilota and Pincoya (*below*) bring drowned sailors to *el Caleuche*?

Many stories surround *el Caleuche* and its crew. One popular tale is that the sailors on the ship were once lost at sea. The stories say that these men were found by the ship and brought on board. Some people even believe that water spirits are responsible for calling the lost sailors to *el Caleuche*.

Chapter 2

NO LONGER SHIPWRECKED

Some phantom ships are believed to be the ghosts of ships that reappeared after having been lost in brutal storms. Witnesses recall seeing a ship sink as waves swamped the decks. Then, sometime later, the very same ship is spotted sailing the sea!

We don't know for sure where phantom ships come from. What do some people believe?

Wintry Shipwreck Spotted Once More

In 1878, the British naval frigate HMS *Eurydice* appeared to sink in a sudden snowstorm. A few parts of the mighty warship were actually recovered, including the ship's bell. Yet through the years, there have been countless sightings of the *Eurydice* sailing around, looking as good as new.

The *Eurydice* sank just off the coast of England.

Britain's Prince Edward is said to have seen the ghostly ship *Eurydice*.

In the 1930s, a Royal Navy submarine commander was worried when he saw the HMS *Eurydice* suddenly appear in front of his submarine. He quickly steered his sub away, only to watch the *Eurydice* vanish before the two ships could collide.

One of the most famous people to see the *Eurydice* was Prince Edward, the son of Britain's Queen Elizabeth II. The prince reportedly caught a glimpse of the ship while filming a documentary in 1998.

Fact or Fiction?

Can a ship really sail across wide oceans after the captain and crew have died?

Believe it or not, it's a fact!

In 1775, a whaling ship discovered a missing British ship called the *Octavius* in the Arctic Ocean, thousands of miles from where it was last known to be traveling. It had been *thirteen years* since the last entry in the captain's log! Everyone on board was frozen. The captain was still sitting at his desk, posed as if writing in his log dated November 11, 1762. How did the ship travel so far without its crew? Could it be that the men aboard the ship navigated it even after their deaths?

The *Octavius* was thought to have been frozen in ice, stranding its crew and leading to their deaths.

A Crash Few Survived

About thirty years after the HMS *Eurydice* first disappeared, a different ship sank in a storm and then mysteriously reappeared many times over the years. On January 22, 1906, the SS *Valencia* was making its way from San Francisco to Seattle when it hit a nasty storm. The *Valencia*'s crew accidentally steered the liner into a reef near Vancouver Island.

With the ship damaged, passengers tried to escape aboard lifeboats. The tragedy continued as three of the boats capsized. By the end of the disaster, 136 people had been killed and only 37 survived.

The remains of one of the *Valencia*'s surviving lifeboats is on display at a maritime museum.

That cold January night took many lives, but it wasn't the last anyone saw of the boat. Through the years, sailors and witnesses on land have looked out at the waters off Vancouver Island and seen the *Valencia* sinking again. They even report seeing crew members and passengers try to hold on against the crashing waves.

Have witnesses really seen a sinking ship just off the coast of Vancouver Island?

HAS A SKELETON CREW BEEN SAILING ALL THIS TIME?

The *Valencia*'s lifeboats may have also reappeared. Not long after the wreck, local American Indians and fishermen reported seeing a lifeboat rowed by skeletons along Vancouver Island's coast. Could it be that the capsized lifeboats became ghost boats, spending the next century trying to escape that deadly storm?

Chapter 3

FLAMING SHIPS

Some of the most legendary ghost ships don't appear as unharmed by their journeys as others. In fact, some ghost ships appear to be on fire! Visions of these flaming vessels have haunted witnesses on rivers, lakes, and even the open ocean for centuries.

Some ghost ships appear to be on fire! Where have people seen them?

Ghost Ship of the Northumberland Strait

For more than 220 years, countless observers have reported seeing a huge sailing ship surrounded by flames in the Northumberland Strait in eastern Canada. Some witnesses say a ball of fire hangs over the ship. Others say they can hear the sound of cannon fire nearby.

Have you ever seen a ship with glowing fire over its sails?

Lifeboats cannot save the lives lost on the burning ship of Northumberland Strait.

Some people have seen the burning ghost ship of Northumberland Strait so clearly that they have made attempts to rescue the crew! In 1900, the craft was spotted by a group of mariners in Prince Edward Island's Charlottetown Harbour. They sent a small boat toward the ship to bring back any survivors. But as the lifeboat got closer, the phantom fire ship disappeared.

Fact or Fiction?

Could moonlight be what's really behind some ghost ship sightings?

It's uncertain.

Some scientists believe that moonlight on the water may cast an eerie glow to convince sailors that a ghost ship is approaching. They say the famous burning ship of the Northumberland Strait may be moonlight reflecting on the thick fog that often hangs over the water. So are ghost ship sightings simply visions of everyday things made more visible in bright light? Or does the moonlight somehow make ghost ships more active? No one can say for sure.

Is this ghostly ship real or a trick of the moonlight?

Tragedy on the River

The twisting Tombigbee River in Alabama may have a ghost ship of its own. On March 1, 1858, the steamboat *Eliza Battle* caught fire near a bend known as Kemp's Landing. Rumors spread that a thief had started the blaze. Others believe sparks from a passing steamboat jumped to the *Eliza Battle*, setting it on fire. Whatever the cause, the ship burned long into the night and was lost forever . . . or so it seemed.

The *Eliza Battle* traveled up and down the Tombigbee River in the 1850s.

In the many years since that tragic night, people on the river and onshore have seen the *Eliza Battle* still burning away. Witnesses have reported hearing music and the sound of people yelling for help coming from the burning ship. Visions of the *Eliza Battle* continuing on its journey south toward Mobile, Alabama, are still reported.

Chapter 4

GHOST SHIPS ON SCHEDULE

Some ghost ships don't appear randomly. Instead, people claim that they can predict the ships' returns. These regular appearances often draw curious people to the spots where the ghost ships tend to come into view.

Ghost ships are mysterious. But can you ever predict when they may appear?

The Reappearing Ship

Some people think the legendary British ship *Lady Lovibond* has made an appearance off the shore of Kent, England, every fifty years since it was wrecked in 1748. The story goes that the ship's captain was murdered and the *Lady Lovibond* got stuck on a sandbank.

Reports say that in 1798, 1848, and 1948, the doomed ship reappeared, only to crash and sink again. Visitors still go to the shore on fifty-year anniversaries, hoping for a glimpse.

Although there have been no recent reports, people still gather in hopes of spotting the *Lady Lovibond*.

Wintry Returns

Another ghost ship that seems to make regular appearances is the *Princess Augusta*. It shows up on the Saturday between Christmas and New Year's Day in the icy waters near Block Island, Rhode Island. The

legendary ship wrecked shortly after Christmas 1738. Witnesses say that a year later, a glowing *Princess Augusta* arrived again. People have said that it reappears every year as a reminder of that December disaster.

> Some legends say that many passengers on the *Princess Augusta* died earlier in their journey from sickness or starvation. The remaining passengers were thought to be killed in the fiery crash.

Fact or Fiction?

Historians sometimes go looking for famous ghost ships.

Fact . . . sort of.

Historians look through documents and records to find the truth behind these mysterious appearances. Some local historians even keep track of local ghost ship sightings. Scientists also study how the original ships may have been lost at sea. Even treasure hunters have searched for the remains of the *Lady Lovibond, Princess Augusta,* and other ships in hopes of finding valuable remains. Divers search underwater in areas where witnesses swear the ghost ships appear. But even with all of this hunting, ghost ships remain a mystery.

Divers search for anchors, treasure, or any other artifacts of disappearing ghost ships.

Any sailor who has spent a lot of time on the water might have a story of seeing something mysterious or unexplainable. Maybe it was a tall sailing ship that vanished in the fog. Perhaps it was a burning ship far away. Or maybe it was a ghost ship making its regular visit to the place where it sank. No one can say where these vessels go, but maybe one day you will go searching for a ghost ship and find one *before* it disappears!

Are tales of ghost ships true? What do you think?

Believe It or Not!

- The *Sea Bird* is a famous ghost ship that sailed into the waters around Rhode Island in 1750 with only a live dog and cat. Coffee was still boiling on a stove.

- A ship called the *Western Reserve* sank off the coast of Michigan in 1892. Only days before the shipwreck, a man called Captain Benjamin Truedell dreamed about the accident.

- The *Mary Celeste* was found floating in the Atlantic Ocean in 1872, after only being at sea for a month. It was perfectly fit to sail, but its crew and captain had vanished.

Glossary

anniversary: the annual date of a special event

capsize: turn over in the water

frigate: a fast naval vessel of the eighteenth and nineteenth centuries

lifeboat: a small boat attached to the side of a ship that can be used to get passengers to safety if the ship is sinking

mariner: a sailor who is usually directly involved in navigation and steering a ship

phantom: a ghost

Royal Navy: the United Kingdom's main naval fighting force

strait: a narrow waterway connecting two large bodies of water

water spirit: a magical creature, such as a mermaid, said to live in the ocean

witness: a person who sees an event happen

wreck: a crash, often of a boat or other vehicle

Learn More about Ghost Ships

Books

Cox, Barbara G., and Scott Forbes. *Wicked Waters*. New York: Gareth Stevens, 2014. Explore some of the most chilling tales of ghost ships in this exciting read.

Gould, Jane H. *The Flying Dutchman*. New York: PowerKids, 2015. Learn more about the most famous ghost ship of them all!

Montgomerie, Adrienne. *Ghost Ships*. New York: Crabtree, 2013. This awesome collection of ghost ship stories will take you from the Bermuda Triangle to a Colorado desert!

Websites

"Ghost Ships: Ten Scary Spirits of the Seven Seas"
http://weburbanist.com/2010/01/31/ghost-ships-ten-scary-spirits-of-the-seven-seas
Ten stories of mysterious ghost ships from throughout history.

"How Do You Find a Ghost Ship?"
http://www.bbc.com/future/story/20140123-how-do-you-find-a-ghost-ship
Discover how scientists and historians search the oceans for ghost ships, and find out what, if anything, is ever recovered.

Scary for Kids: *Flying Dutchman*
http://www.scaryforkids.com/flying-dutchman
Check out this site to learn more about the *Flying Dutchman* and about books and movies based on the ship's spooky legend!

Index

el Caleuche, 9–10

Eliza Battle, 22–23

Flying Dutchman, 5–7

HMS *Eurydice*, 12–13, 15

Lady Lovibond, 25, 27

lifeboat, 15, 17, 20

Northumberland Strait, 19–21

Princess Augusta, 26–27

rescue, 20

skeleton, 5, 17

SS *Valencia*, 15–17

Photo Acknowledgments

The images in this book are used with the permission of: © Look and Learn/Bridgeman Images, p. 4; © Walt Disney/Courtesy Everett Collection, p. 5; © PsychoShadow/Shutterstock.com, p. 6; © Antiqua Print Gallery/Alamy, p. 7; © Johannes Gerhardus Swanepoel/Dreamstime.com, p. 8; © Andrey_Kuzmin/Shutterstock.com, p. 9; © iStockphoto.com/Lena_graphics, p. 10; © iStockphoto.com/andrzej5003, p. 11; © iStockphoto.com/guenterguni, p. 12; © Stephen Barnes/UK/Alamy, p. 13; © iStockphoto.com/duncan1890, pp. 14, 20; © David Wei/Alamy, p. 15; © iStockphoto.com/Sjo, p. 16; © Dorling Kindersley/Getty Images, p. 17; © iStockphoto.com/nightman1965, p. 18; © Galushko Sergey/Shutterstock.com, p. 19; © Melkor3D/Shutterstock.com, p. 21; © Niday Picture Library/Alamy, p. 22; © Thomas Escher/dieKleinert/Alamy, p. 23; © iStockphoto.com/JamesBrey, p. 24; © Aleksey Sagitov/Shutterstock.com, p. 25; © North Wind Picture Archives/Alamy, p. 26; © iStockphoto.com/Tammy616, p. 27; © PLRANG ART/Shutterstock.com, p. 28.

Front cover: © Alfredo Schaufelberger/Shutterstock.com.

Main body text set in Adrianna Regular 14/20.
Typeface provided by Chank.